2013

To Matt,
Blessings to you as you
walk with God.
Love,
Grandma Laurel

EARLY MORNING WALKS WITH GOD

LAUREL STANELL

Inspiring Voices®
A Service of **Guideposts**

Inspiring Voices books may be ordered through booksellers or by contacting:

Inspiring Voices
1663 Liberty Drive
Bloomington, IN 47403
www.inspiringvoices.com
1-(866) 697-5313

ISBN: 978-1-4624-0304-2 (sc)
ISBN: 978-1-4624-0303-5 (e)

Library of Congress Control Number: 2012916890

Printed in the United States of America

Inspiring Voices rev. date: 11/26/2012

Change of Seasons

Laurel Stanell

Here's what I saw
on a walk today:
some feathers all ready
to blow away.

Bark from some trees,
leaves that were blowing,
feathers like plumes,
broken but flowing.

Pine needles that dropped
after changing to brown,
pieces of pinecones
that fell to the ground.

A smashed sycamore "cone"
with points still in view,
dried flowers on a bush
not showing a hue.

All of these pieces were shed
for a reason:
to make ready for growth
and change of a season.

And people have changes
of seasons too,
when they shed some ideas
and think something new.

It's a gradual growth
every day, every year,
but no need to worry,
God's always there.

Introduction

On my daily early morning walks around the lake and by a golf course where I live, thoughts came to me from which I drew analogies that relate these experiences to God's promises.

Laurel Stanell, Whispering Pines, North Carolina

January

January 1

It was later than usual by two hours, so the sun was bright. What a great day for the first day of the year. Thoughts of resolutions had been on TV and in the newspapers for the New Year. Thank God that He gives us the chance to start again anytime, every day, as we ask for forgiveness and turn ourselves over to Him.

January 2

Christmas tree lights were still on the docks around the lake. This may have been the last day. When they are put away, they'll be missed. How comforting to know that the everlasting light will always be with us in Jesus Christ.

January 3

The whole beautiful day stretched out to be full of what God had planned. There were decorations to be taken down, but there were also neighbors and friends who might have needed a special touch of food, conversation, or just a greeting. God always directs.

January 4

The sky was full of clouds—gray from last night's rain, white on the edges, blue in space—and the sun's rays, inching their way across the east. God painted scenes with these clouds, in which I saw an island surrounded by mountains, a river, and an eye that seemed to watch over all—just as God watches over all.

January 5

The balmy wind—unusual for this time of year—blew through the trees as I walked. The unusual happens every day, and God is there to help us through unexpected events as He sees fit.

January 6

This morning, a military man I've talked with many times was walking his well-behaved dog. We exchanged greetings, and he told me about his family visiting for the holidays and a birthday. He had been to Afghanistan and was anticipating a trip to Iraq. How fortunate that God provides help through many people in many ways. Am I listening to how He will send me to help today?

January 7

The sun was showing its light. Gradually, it became brighter until the whole sky was invaded with light. That is how God came into my life—gradually. As a child, I was just learning about Him through Bible stories, parents, and friends and then experiencing the awareness of prayers being answered. As an adult, I have realized His being in me is the one thing I can turn to. I can let His light invade my being.

January 8

The moon stayed bright and full even after the sun started to lighten the sky. I noticed the sharp shadows, which soon changed direction and disappeared into the light. In life, our *shadows* change direction and disappear as the light from God overtakes them.

January 9

Snow was over all, as large and small snowflakes hit the ground and me. Recently, I read about the intricacy of each snowflake and thought of our complex bodies, where our spirits dwell. If God gives so much to the working of each snowflake, imagine how much He gives to us to live. That doesn't even compare to our spirits that can live eternally with Him if we believe in Christ Jesus.

January 10

Winter wonderland was with us, with puffy snow on the trees. Only one other person was walking, and she was coming with a dog. It was so beautiful; I wondered why others weren't out enjoying it. God knows their reasons, just as He knows why they're holding back instead of coming and believing in His Son.

January 11

So many mailboxes; so much information received. Will it be something to pay, toss, or keep? Will it be friendly? Every day, we must sort and make decisions about what is worth keeping. Isn't that what life is about—receiving mail and sorting out what is worthwhile for God's glory?

January 12

A car went by, and all of a sudden I was casting several shadows caused by the car, moon, and streetlight, all in different locations. God knows how many *shadows* or *light* we send out each day to the people we meet. May God help us give out *light* in His name rather than *shadows*.

January 13

I met a neighbor early on the walk this morning. We commented on the beautiful moon casting much light. He said it would follow me. That's just as Christ Jesus follows me—all the time. How fortunate to have that constant light!

January 14

The road was dark in spots this morning because the moon was hidden. At times, I stumbled on some unseen rough spots. Without God's light, we will *stumble*, but then the seemingly hidden light will come again as promised to help keep us from *stumbling*.

January 15

The dark morning was made lighter by the moon. As I neared the area where a couple might be walking their three large dogs, I was on heightened alert so as to be on the opposite side. As we face life daily, Satan is always trying to get us to walk in his path so he can overcome us. Praise to God for helping us be alert to God's way that protects us.

January 16

The hymn "Praise God from Whom All Blessings Flow" kept running through my mind on the walk this morning. Early beauty of the morning, neighbors, friends, church, good health—so many blessings for which to praise God all day long.

January 17

The morning was chilly, and someone had a fire. There was smoke in the air—enough to make me feel warm inside just thinking about it. Sometimes we have *smoke* in our lives that covers something good, and sometimes it covers something bad. God knows the good *smoke* we have and how much bad *smoke* we can take.

January 18

In the dark morning hours, a neighbor was startled when he came out for the paper and heard me say, "Good morning." How many times do we startle people? Are our words and actions always intended for good, or is it sometimes not so good? God is there to guide us to the good.

January 19

A neighbor up the street was walking her dog. I hadn't seen her in a while, but true to form, the dog rolled over to be scratched on the belly—a habit from way back. Do we have habits from way back? Some are good; some are bad. With God's help, we can overcome the bad.

January 20

First thing out the door this morning, I heard a lone bird squawking loudly. Gradually, that diminished, and other birds began chirping. Daily, we meet squawkers and chirpers who work with life differently. God is there for all of us, and if we ask Him for help, He'll work with us and help us find peace through the squawking and the chirping.

January 21

A piercing front light that just turned on was flashing. That meant the police or emergency was called. Sure enough, the police came as I walked by. God is there for us in trouble. He'll help us even when we may not know enough to send "signals," but He does want us to communicate and be in touch with Him all the time.

January 22

Smoke was coming out of a heat pump at a neighbor's house. Since fires can start in heat pumps, I paused and watched from the street and decided to inform the neighbors. Just as I was walking up to their door, the pump went off, and the smoke disappeared. In our daily lives, God is there when we're checking through "smoke" to see what's causing it. He'll see us through, no matter what the cause. What a comfort!

January 23

The morning was beautiful—nothing unsettling about the cold temps that the four layers of clothing couldn't handle. Still, I felt unsettled inside after an unsettling week. At the end of the walk, I met a neighbor, and we greeted and commented on the beauty in the cold. By then, I was warm and expressed comfort. God gets us warmed up for our activities, and He wants us to be patient and follow His steps. He will comfort us in our unsettled feelings in His time.

January 24

Everywhere, there was beautiful sunlight; everywhere, there were the beautiful works of God. Thank You, God, for all the beauty and for Jesus Christ, the light!

January 25

Only one star—maybe a planet—was shining early this morning. As I saw all the tumultuous clouds that were to bring sleet and snow later in the day, I wondered how that one shining light could appear in the midst of it all. But that's like our life. In the midst of our turmoil, we have the one bright light of Christ that shines through it all.

January 26

Blue markers on the road directed the meter readers to the water meters at each house. Do we need markers to let it be known that we are Christians, or can people find us without a marker? God is with us when He directs them to our door.

January 27

A neighbor with a cane came out to retrieve the newspaper on the ice. She saw me and asked if I would pick it up for her. Since she wobbled on her own, I carried it to the door and gave it to her. God puts us in the right place at the right time. How do we respond?

January 28

Stepping out on the icy street this morning, I noticed many sparkles just ahead. Directly behind me, the sun was rising, producing the sparkles all around. Those sparkles that reflected the light from behind made me think Christ is here to give "sparkles" to our future, even if we've momentarily turned our backs on the light.

January 29

There were pages of the morning paper blown along the road. At first I passed by, but then I went and picked them up. Pieces of our lives are in disarray many times. Do we stop and pick them up or ask for help in picking them up before going on? Do we help others pick up their pieces? Listen to God, who nudges us to act and help where we can.

January 30

The rain was steady, but the umbrella covered me. Oh, yes, the feet got a little wet, but nothing compared to what could have been had I not been protected. God covers us when troubles rain. He is our umbrella.

January 31

The fog was dense, which made the dark seem darker, but just when light was needed, a streetlight came on. God's light is always there—especially when our way is *dark and foggy.* Seek it, and relinquish your darkness to Him.

February

February 1

The umbrella was in hand, although there was no rain—at first. Then it came, and the protection was there. In our daily lives "rain" doesn't always come first thing, but when it comes, God is there to cover and protect us.

February 2

The sky was very dark with thick clouds. Within the forty-five minute walk, it was light, with the sun coming up behind those thick clouds. The sun couldn't be seen, but the light was there. We can count on God's light penetrating our *darkness*. We just have to be patient and wait for His time to brighten our lives.

February 3

Bright pink and white puffs of clouds with blue in between filled the area of sky where the sun was emerging. On the opposite side were long clouds with different, softer blends. The lake reflected it all. What beauty God gives to us to enjoy.

February 4

Many times we have to change our course because of our circumstances, but God, because of His love, doesn't change His course of guidance. All we have to do is ask for this guidance to *weather* any storm.

February 5

Darkness covered the road, but turning and looking through the tall pines, I saw a bright light that penetrated and sparkled. Many times we seem to be in total darkness, but if we turn ourselves toward God, His light will penetrate our very beings and cause us to *sparkle* in our darkness.

February 6

The sky was just beginning to get light in the early morning. As I looked into the still dark trees, I noticed lights on one that almost looked like Christmas lights. However, they were just streaks of lights coming through trees across the way. Christ comes to us with His light when everything else seems dark. He can come to us through other people, through various circumstances, when we are making decisions, and when we are asking for help. Thank You, Christ, for Your light.

February 7

Guidelines are painted along the sides and middle of the road. They are so familiar that sometimes we don't even see them; we just keep going anyway. Perhaps we miss them most when road resurfacing is being done and there are no lines yet to guide us. God gives us guidelines for all "conditions." Do we seek and then follow them?

February 8

Footprints startled the skinny, blue heron as it stalked near the lake. Suddenly, the wide wings spread, and off it went to safer ground. How comforting that God is there with His wings to protect us and that they're always open.

February 9

An empty cigarette package was in the middle of the road, garbage for one to pick up so it doesn't get spread about. As we move about, we may hear, see, or pick up some "garbage," but God is there to help us not to "spread it."

February 10

Red reflectors are in place at some driveways along the way. However, they only reflect in the dark with a spot of brightness to guide us. Are we reflectors of God's way to those who come our way? Do we bring a "spot" of brightness along uncertain paths?

February 11

The bark on one tree was all stripped down in a heap on the ground around a tree. A thought came that the tree was just like life. We peel away parts of our lives and go on. There is a saying, "Life is like an onion: you peel away one layer at a time, and sometimes you cry." God is with us in all of life's "peelings."

February 12

The police car passed by during the pre-dawn hours. How comforting to know the patrolling was for our protection. Even more comforting is knowing God is always protecting us.

February 13

I passed at least fifty driveways and only one vehicle that was actually being driven first thing this morning. Then, by one driveway, a truck was coming that wanted to turn in, and we both stopped. The driver waved me on. Daily, we must be prepared for the unexpected to cross our paths. God will help us with every obstacle.

February 14

Gray clouds covered the sky. All of a sudden, the sun peaked through—the bright spot. Our days may be gray, but if we give them a chance, the light of God is there—the bright spot peaking through the gray.

February 15

Pansies were bright and colorful in mid-winter when many things gray and dull were in various yards. Are we a touch of brightness when things seem gray and dull around us? With God's help, we can be.

February 16

Sand, gravel, pods, cones, leaves, dirt, grass, weeds, and much more covered the ground—all for different purposes. Isn't that the way with us? All here, all different, and all for different purposes. What does God have in store for us?

February 17

The road surface was so frozen that footprints didn't show. However, one could walk on the shoulders where feet could pierce the ground and make a print. Sometimes we can't leave our *prints* on our *circumstances*, but if we search through God, He will guide us to the surface that will carry our prints.

February 18

Ice covered the trees, individual pine needles, leaves, cones, branches, and buds all along the way. All were individual, and the overall scene seemed frozen in time, but growth continued on the inside. Perhaps it would be God's direction that life on the outside would seem frozen to give us time to grow on the inside.

February 19

The moon was sifting in and out of the clouds, so there was a light spot in the sky as well as a reflection cast on a puddle. The moon's light is a reflection from the sun as we are reflections of God. Do we cast a reflection of God to others?

February 20

Mud was splattered across the road where a vehicle had veered off and caught the wet shoulders. Do we sometimes veer off course and scatter *mud* up our road? God can set our course on the solid road again.

February 21

An arrow with "Open House" printed on it points the way to a house up a street. It's a place where people can go and perhaps negotiate to buy. God has a house too. He wants you to come and look and ask and talk to Him about it anytime.

February 22

Branches that had broken and fallen were barely hanging onto the limbs below. Do we barely *hang on* at times? The difference is that we're not dead, and God is there to lift us up.

February 23

Rain, sleet, and snow hit us last night, but the roads weren't frozen, so a walk was possible. It was interesting to note in the dark that some lawns were all white with snow or frost while others had no white. It's as if God was selective—just as He is with people. He loves us all, but He does give us different gifts and asks us to use them for Him for His different tasks.

February 24

Frost on the golf course, mist rising from the lake, blue sky, partial moon, beautiful sunrise, and last week's mud washed from the road from downpours are all part of God's power. He is powerful in our lives, and we can feel it, as we're open to it.

February 25

Even the birds weren't out at this early hour. How still! And how dark. However, lights were being turned on, and the usual dog walkers were out. When I turned in the driveway, I heard the first bird and then others, almost as if a welcoming committee were there. Won't it be great when we get to heaven and have our family and friends with God welcoming us?

February 26

Because of the thick cloud cover, there were neither stars nor a moon to be seen, but there was an overall glow and, especially the reflection from the nearby airport. Sometimes we may not see individual "lights" in our lives, but in communion with God there is a constant spiritual glow.

February 27

Brown, slippery pine straw covered the roadsides along the way. In the midst of it, there was a white rock by a driveway. What a contrast! There is usually at least one bright "rock" each day to contrast with whatever is *overwhelming, slippery, or dull*. God gives us bright spots to keep us going. Thank You, God.

February 28

Rushing water was trying to squeeze through drainage pipes on both ends of the lake after yesterday's heavy rain. Do we feel squeezed inside when events have pummeled our insides? Do we ask God to help calm those insides? He will bring the peace.

February 29

A school bus, maintenance truck, and a serviceman were the only three to pass by on the walk this morning. Education, taking care of our surroundings, and protection in the world were the three things that came to mind. And who can give us guidance in these three? God.

March

March 1

Pine trees were standing tall and straight after the recent ice storm and melting. One small tree was still bent way over and needed help if it were to straighten out. In our lives, circumstances cause us to bend. Children need guidance to grow straight, and all of us need support wires. God is our constant support.

March 2

Mud was on the shoulder along a short stretch, and a car was coming. There was no other place to step to get off the road. Sometimes we step in *mud* to get out of the way of something worse. Thankfully, God is there to get us back on clean ground.

March 3

Vines with branches climbing high were covering many trees and stumps in one area along the way. If it weren't for a strong vine, the branches would not have nourishment, and without branches, the vine could go undetected. As Jesus said, He is our vine, and we are the branches. He gives us the nourishment for us to proclaim Him in this world.

March 4

Garbage cans are out one of two days a week. Imagine getting rid of the scraps only two days a week that we don't want any longer. We can get rid of the "garbage" inside ourselves that we don't want by confessing to God about the "junk" we carry, and He'll clean it up anytime.

March 5

The moisture in the air felt like rain, but I could see no drops on the puddles of water along the way. My hair and coat were damp but not soaking. Don't we sometimes feel something there along our way and yet can't see it happening? Maybe God just wants to sharpen our senses so we can feel the invisible as well as the visible. He'll be there for all the "feelings."

March 6

A pickup truck was rounding a corner, crossed over the center line, and came straight at me. Fortunately, it turned left at the corner and went onto the causeway. Do we ever think disaster is coming right at us and then it turns? God is there, watching and protecting us.

March 7

No vehicles passed me on the first half of the walk. It was so peaceful. Then several vehicles came rushing by on their way to work at the golf club. How many times is our peace interrupted as we are rushing to work, events, meeting someone, and so on? Do we rush to do God's work as well? Do we keep up our communication with Him so we can hear what He would like us to do in our rushing?

March 8

Garden club members were pruning crape myrtle bushes along the causeway to stimulate new growth. Our lives also need *pruning* to stimulate new growth for what God wants us to do. Having someone else to work with helps the pruning also.

March 9

The first Sunday edition of the local newspaper was in the middle of the driveway at 5:30 a.m. How many firsts have we had in our lives? Every day brings them, but there are momentous ones and some we don't even remember, such as taking our first steps. However, talking with God is the first step we should consciously take every day.

March 10

Mist drops were in the air. They couldn't be seen, but I felt them. I put up the umbrella, but the moisture came underneath. Sometimes we can feel things but not see them. God sent His Holy Spirit to feel and then do His will. We may not *see* the things to be done, but we can *feel* them.

March 11

Birds were chirping loudly in different "languages." Do they understand each other's language, or do they just hear the noise? Do we understand each other, or do we just hear the words and noise? God is with us and can help us communicate with each other. In turn, we can follow His command and lead to help and love others as they express their needs.

March 12

The fog was dense, which made the dark seem darker. But just when light was needed, a lamppost turned on. When our way is *dark and foggy*, God's light is there. He gave us His son Jesus as our light to guide us. It's there to seek.

March 13

A neighbor had a small banner with a brightly colored design of a watering can and flowers on display. Spring is coming! Soon the beautiful and varied designs full of colors that God provides will be in full bloom—with fragrances!

March 14

What will be new today? I thought this as I walked out the door. Right away there was a greeting from a dog, a young couple, and another dog that I had never met before. Morning greetings were exchanged. Be prepared! Be prepared for all newness that God has in store.

March 15

Two ducks swam out from the shore into the cold water. Rain permeated the air, but none of this changed the ducks; they were protected with the same "clothes." God takes care of their needs, and they go about their lives. Likewise, He takes care of our needs and us.

March 16

To take the umbrella or not . . . even though the air is just moist, maybe it'll really start raining soon. Sure enough, it came down about a third of the way around the lake. Do we heed those inner callings of our Lord? Those that give us opportunities to serve Him? They're with us, and we just have to be still and listen.

March 17

A black cat was flat on the ground and looking at me as if to say, "If I'm quiet you won't see me—or see what I just did." Do we play the same game with the Lord? Do we think He won't see what we just did—or what we are planning to do? He knows our every move, which is why Jesus came, died, and was resurrected—so that we might live like He did and be saved through grace even though our actions aren't perfect.

March 18

Paths wind off through the woods around the lake. How many paths have we taken that led us to where we are, and how many were not taken? We have choices, and with God's guidance we can take the path He wishes us to take.

March 19

The moon was almost full, the sun was coming up, the sky was clear, and many flowers were open. This was visible, all in spite of an uncertain winter and predictions of rain yesterday and today. God is in control no matter what weather is anticipated.

March 20

Four ducks were swimming on the lake this morning, one female and three males. All of a sudden, the three males were fighting and one left the group—rejected. We face rejection in our lives but not with God. He'll receive those who come to Him, and we'll be with His people forever.

March 21

This is the first day of spring. Just as God brings changes in the seasons of the year, He gives us changes in the seasons of our lives. Sometimes there is color and cloudless skies; sometimes it's drab with clouds closing in. Whatever the "weather" in our lives, He's there to help us through our "change of seasons."

March 22

Flowering trees were bursting all around the area, but there were still some in tight buds getting ready. It's a good example of everything in due season. God is with us as our lives unfold from buds to bursting forth.

March 23

A truck piled with lumber was at the village hall. *What will be built with that?* I wondered. Although I didn't have lumber, I wondered what I'd *build* today. Would it be something I felt God was nudging me to do? Big or small, with a prayer He'll be right there, guiding the action.

March 24

The sky was clear and getting brighter with the light from the rising sun. The partial moon was still visible, even though there was brightness all around. Does my life reflect the light from Jesus even through some of the worldly lights are overwhelming?

March 25

Walks to the front doors of neighbors vary. Some are straight, some have steps, some are curved, and some may be off the driveway. To get into the houses, it may be more convenient to go to the side or back doors. Our hearts are like that. We may have various paths to reaching people's hearts with God's love. In fact, some may have their doors locked no matter what path we take. All we can do is try.

March 26

A police car was parked along the side of the road, no doubt to catch speeders as they rushed to their destination. Do we speed through our daily lives, or do we slow down to enjoy what God gives to us every day?

March 27

A neighbor was out walking his dog and expressed feeling guilty (which he usually does) about not walking around the lake each morning. Do we feel and maybe express a feeling because of something we've done or didn't do? It's a good thing God sent His son, a savior who took our guilt with Him and also listens to us when we ask forgiveness for our daily felt guilt.

March 28

A train whistle was in the distance, a plane was overhead, a car was on a nearby street—all of these sounds so identifiable. Do we hear the Lord and clearly identify Him when He's drawing our attention? Or is He mixed in with all the worldly noises?

March 29

The individual reflectors between the double yellow lines in the center of the road were worn down and needed to be replaced. Are our "reflectors" of God down and in need of replacement? For our asking He provides daily renewal.

March 30

The only ones out this rainy Sunday morning were a couple walking three dogs, something they must do every day. There are things we must do every day that are easy, and there are also things we must do that are a burden. God will see us through our burdens if we turn them over to Him.

March 31

Sycamore balls were strewn along the way. Some were still perfect, and some were roughed up. Do we have days that we feel were perfect and other days that were roughed up? God is with us through it all and appreciates our thanks for the perfect as well as the growth that comes during the rough times.

April

April 1

The sky was overcast and the ground wet from the night's rain. But—the Bradford pear trees were in full bloom! At the corner, the streetlight made a tree noticeably glow. Do we have a noticeable glow from the light of Christ, either on a "still corner" or along a "busy highway"?

April 2

At the entrance of a few driveways there is surface that is pressed to look like brick—an imitation. How many of us are imitators of the world rather than seekers of God's will for our real selves? We are directed to be in and not of the world.

April 3

The sky was blue with white clouds, the sun bright, and all of a sudden, there were raindrops. Looking up, I saw a thin, gray mist-like cloud above me. Our bright days might be like that all of a sudden. God is there through it all.

April 4

Yellow-green pine pollen permeates the earth and penetrates unsecured places. God also covers the earth, as does Satan. Which one are you going to ask to penetrate your heart? Both would like to be there, but it's up to you to decide.

April 5

At least half of the vehicles that passed me by this morning had drivers using cell phones. If our world would be in communication with God the same amount of time, how much better we would be!

April 6

A flowering tree that had dripping, pink blossoms was faded out this morning. Do our "flowering" ways fade out also? As we keep close to Jesus, He will guide us into new growth and flowers.

April 7

A neighbor came out and greeted me in a cheery voice. He's so upbeat and keeps going in spite of having been diagnosed with cancer about a year ago and deciding on no treatment. God is truly showing through him as He does in marvelous ways all the time.

April 8

My thoughts were in getting ready for the family coming next week for Easter: decorating, cleaning, treasure hunts, etc. What a setting for thoughts, with the trees and flowers blossoming in all colors. God has given us many kinds of treasures. The all-important one is His son Jesus Christ, the focal point of Easter.

April 9

A cat came straight at me this morning—unusual. Most cats run away, but this one wasn't afraid. As we face people, God will be there too to help us with any fears. Just ask Him and listen.

April 10

This morning was sunny and brisk, with beautiful blossoms on the trees in the yards all around. What a start to a day, walking in God's world with all this beauty that He's provided.

April 11

Many trees have been cut down around the golf courses, and stumps are left. A buzzing sound could be heard as someone was leveling a stump. Back and forth went the buzz saw as chips went flying. Do we have "stumps" to remove in our lives? God promises to be with us in all our trials, and He'll be there to give us comfort and strength as we remove our "stumps."

April 12

New posts were placed where the old, rotten ones along the causeway had been pulled. The wood is so shinny, and the grain and knots are so prevalent. When our old ways have been pulled and beautiful new ones are put in place, do we feel refreshed? When Christ is leading our lives, the old is gone and the new is in us. Thank You, God, for making us live refreshed.

April 13

The moon was setting as the sun was rising on the other side of the lake. The sun and moon give us the light to brighten up the day and night, and Christ gives us the light to brighten up our insides. He is the brightest light of the world for our walks in life.

April 14

Pine pollen covers everything, and my tracks can be seen up the asphalt driveway more than any other place around the house. Throughout our lives, we leave many "tracks", some good and some bad. God is with us to help us make "tracks" in His name—the good ones that help other people.

April 15

Purple wildflowers were standing tall and reaching for the light. The maintenance man was coming with a mower to cut them down, but they will come up again. This is Holy Week, when we're reminded that Jesus stood tall and then was cut down—or so thought the world. However, He rose again. That's good news!

April 16

A lone golf ball was in the grass along the causeway. Since it was in the wrong direction from the golf course, I speculated that how it got there was either a hook off the tee or that it fell from someone's golf cart. Sometimes we *hit* what we had hoped would be a good shot but find ourselves off the course. God is there to help us make "straight shots."

April 17

My walk today was with three family members from out of town. The sun was up, and the spring trees were in full bloom. How great to share all of this with others and hear their appreciation of the spring beauty. How blessed we are! Do we thank God enough for all He has given to us? Probably not!

April 18

The birds were chirping wildly first thing out the door this morning. They didn't harmonize but seemed to give solos, one after another with their greetings. People don't always harmonize either, for they each need solo time. God hears it all, and as we ask for His guidance and listen, we can respond in His will with our solos or harmonizing.

April 19

A large branch with pinecones was dangling from a wire. How will it free itself? Do we find our lives on *wires*, not sure of the outcome? God will take care of us. He will free us.

April 20

A plane flew overhead from the small airport nearby. Imagine—being about to fly! For our planes, it's been just more than one hundred years. But for thousands of years birds, butterflies, other insects, etc., have all been flying and helping God with nature in many ways. What a world God made!

April 21

Clink. A new golf cup hole was dug on the green and the flag replaced as I walked by the golf course. Here was a new challenge. How many new challenges will be faced today? Wherever they are, God will be there too.

April 22

A house that had been vacant for years has new owners. Trucks, a dumpster, and even a port-o-john have been in the driveway for two months while the interior was being fixed. Now the yard machines are working on the landscape. Do we spend much time *fixing* our insides, or do we leave it for another time?

April 23

Gray or blue skies—which will it be today? Whatever, the day is here to stay. Are events going to be gray, sunny, or a mixture? No matter what, God is with us and will help us see sunshine when we prayerfully seek it.

April 24

The moon was still out this early morning, something not seen through all of these cloudy skies these past two months—how refreshing to see it. God provides many refreshing breakthroughs in our cloudy nights and days—and they're so welcome. Thank You, God.

April 25

Numbers on mailboxes are placed in a variety of ways. Our civil lives depend on numbers to easily bank, receive mail, use credit cards, have phones, pay/receive Social Security, and so on. However, God knows us without numbers. What a comfort!

April 26

"Don't get wet," said a neighbor on the walk this morning—and it wasn't raining. There were darker clouds in the sky, and predictions were for rain later. How many times are we told or do we feel it's implied that we shouldn't get involved or "get wet" in a situation? With God's direction, we can "get wet" if it's in His purpose.

April 27

Yesterday I picked up a black feather from the ground. When I arrived home it wasn't in my pocket. How many times do we lose something and then not find it until suddenly there it is. When we think we've lost God's attention it comes to us to help us in mysterious ways!

April 28

Petals from the dogwood and azaleas were covering the ground as they dropped. One dogwood petal was *walking* as the wind picked it up and moved it along, away from the rest. Do we walk away from the crowd to follow God's will, or do we just walk away to do our own thing and be "me" people? It's our choice.

April 29

A mother duck with several ducklings close to her were swimming, and the father was circling around them for protection. Isn't that what God our Father does for us? Circles around constantly to protect us? How fortunate we are to have that love.

April 30

The small ditch at the top of the driveway was to allow the residue water to drain off before it would run down the driveway and make it harder to get to the house. We can ask God to help us *drain* our unneeded residue so it doesn't get in the way of how He wants us to progress.

May

May 1

Walking by one azalea bush I noticed two pink blossoms in the middle—all else white. It certainly made me pay attention! Christ stands out among all other people in what He did for us. It certainly should make us pay attention.

May 2

This morning the sky looked clear as I started out. About one fourth of the way around, it started to pour. There was distant thunder, which usually scares me, but I prayed a storm wouldn't come, and it didn't. Of course I was soaked but kept thinking *this is an unexpected happening, just like many of our experiences every day.* With God's help we'll be able to cope with each one. What a comfort!

May 3

Debris was strewn all over, but in many places it was clear. The storm last night caused it all. Sometimes a storm can leave our lives messy, but then again, it can blow away a former mess. God will be there when each storm comes, and He will help us see it through.

May 4

Up ahead, a neighbor was walking with a radio plugged into her ears. She didn't hear anything until a loud "Good morning." How many times are we plugged into the world so that we don't hear God? As promised, He's always with us and will hear it all.

May 5

"Tag Sale—come and buy—take it with you"; that's the message that was on a sign as people were getting ready to move. However, we can't buy eternal life with God or take anything with us. He has all that we need. Maybe "Tag Sale" could also mean "*Take After God* (Who) *Saves All Believers Eternally!*"

May 6

Many wildflowers are coloring the roadside. Interesting how some have flowers on just the very top, and some have blossoms down the stem; some are in clusters, and others are standing alone. God made them all to give different beauty, just as God made us all for different beauty. Do we ask Him how we can develop that beauty in His name?

May 7

An early storm kept me from walking before 8:30 church. Thoughts came that I could walk in an indoor facility later. However, the day cleared, and I had more time to walk four instead of three miles around two lakes instead of the usual one. God's scenery is much more beautiful than walls in a building. He always makes it more interesting. We just have to be patient and wait for His timing.

May 8

The sun had been up for close to two hours, but now it was hiding behind a cloud that was very dark in the center, and it couldn't break through. However, the edges were lacy, and sparkly rays were showing beautifully. It made me think how thick the clouds were, just like our inner beings are sometimes so thick that the light of Jesus can't penetrate there yet. However,

He may come through the edges gradually, and the center will break up and let Him come all the way in and through us so we can show His light.

May 9

A pair of ducks waddled across the road from the lake across to a neighbor's yard. When my footsteps were heard, the male and then the female stopped dead still. He was guiding and protecting her by natural instinct. Isn't it a comfort to know that God is guiding and protecting us from potential harm? Thank You, God.

May 10

A black Lab type dog followed me along on the road, apparently lost, tired, and hungry. I took him home, and after I fed him, he took a needed nap. He trusted me. I called the police so the rightful owners could be found. When we're lost, tired, and hungry for whatever, God provides the needed help. We just have to trust Him.

May 11

Clouds grayed the sky all around except for the one bright spot where the sun was trying to show. Even though our skies are gray, there must be one bright spot. Let us look for it and give God thanks for that.

May 12

As promised, the high humidity was gone and the air was clear this morning. That's what God also promises. If there are close, tough times, He will "clear the air" for us and give us peace.

May 13

Magnolia blossoms are out. Interesting how one big flower is beautiful on its own—but so are the clusters of small flowers. God's plan is that sometimes we *shine* for Him on our own and sometimes in groups. It can all work to make life more interesting and beautiful.

May 14

Curves and hills along the way make it hard to see what's up ahead, but I keep going and trust the road will too. Every day we face situations in which we can't see up ahead. Trusting that God is always with us, we can keep going in peace and assurance.

May 15

The bushes along the causeway were quite uniform in their clipping, but in some of them there were different kinds of stems stretching higher than the others. Do we as Christians stretch tall above others so our "differences" are noticed for being more Christlike?

May 16

My mind was so full of trip preparations that I hardly noticed God's beautiful nature that surrounded me; I just kept walking on, making lists. At the end of the walk, I realized what had happened and thanked God that He was still there even if my eyes and mind weren't open to nature's beauty.

May 17

It was slightly later for the walk today. One school bus came by, people walked by, but no one was walking a dog—very unusual. Sometimes we just expect things or take things for granted, and they aren't what we expect. We can depend on God to be there—that's not unusual—but how He wants us to respond to His wishes may be. Do we act the way He would expect us to? Or do we just go through our usual routine and not pay attention to what may be unusual about what He wants from us?

May 18

A neighbor's dog started to walk and pulled toward me on its leash. Oh, if all could be that friendly in greeting one another! It might not always be that accepted; however, God is that friendly. In fact, He constantly has His arms around us. We just have to accept Him.

May 19

A woman's white sweater was in the middle of the road. Someone lost it, so I hung it on a sign where it was easy to see. How often do we lose or misplace something? We're frustrated and spend much time looking for it. When the Good Shepherd loses one of His flock, He's on the constant lookout to find the one that's missing. We are blessed to have this constant vigilance so we can go home with Him.

May 20

Birds come in purple, pink, red, yellow, orange, brown, black, and blue, in all shades and in all mixtures. How could one not believe that God made it all? Creation of this magnitude would be too complicated for human beings, and just chance would take too long. Thank You, God, for the beauty in the variety.

May 21

A woman was getting her paper this morning, and I noticed her face was bruised on one side. We exchanged "Good morning," and on we went. In going beyond, the thought came to me that I hadn't checked if she needed help. How many times do we pass by people who need help—even if they don't ask? May God help keep us alert to do the right thing.

May 22

This morning a neighbor gal who lives several curves from here was walking her dog and called me by my first name. I don't know hers and so just gave a greeting. Then I thought, *God knows all our names, millions of them, and some don't know Him at all.*

May 23

A squirrel was racing up and down and around the branches of a tree, sometime going out on fragile limbs. I thought, *we race like that sometimes on the steady trunk of life or on fragile branches. "Thank you God for being with us as we race, and also for sending Christ as our main trunk of the vine."*

May 24

The walk was slightly later than usual this morning. One neighbor I meet occasionally said, "You're always out early" and meant *how come you're early today too?* Another neighbor said, "How come you're so late?" Perception is interesting and made me wonder how I perceive others and how I've been wrong at times. But God knows us and can perceive what we're like inside—what others can't see.

May 25

There was a constant buzz by the lake, and as I got closer I saw men trimming the bushes. Even though they had on earmuffs, they still heard some noise—but only part of it. Do we only hear the buzz around us in our daily lives, or can we talk and listen to people? Pray that God will help us hear through all the noise.

May 26

Puffy clouds in a contained, oblong shape were reflected in the still lake. I looked up and saw them spread across the sky. Beautiful sight! In retrospect, I thought, *do we often see a reflection first when we encounter a person who reflects a strong faith in Christ?* A person who sees this reflection may be moved to look at the "real" beauty of Christ firsthand, similar to looking at the real clouds in the sky.

May 27

A feather was on the road, so I picked it up and looked at its details. The colors, the fine strands that made it up, and the curved shape served a purpose to the bird. God has shaped us to our last detail, and each part has a purpose. For our overall purpose, we only have to ask Him and listen to the Holy Spirit that He gave us to find out that purpose.

May 28

The pecking of a woodpecker produced a hollow sound. It made me think of Satan pecking away at us and trying to get at our hollow selves—perhaps to fill them up. But with God there, they can't be filled with something else.

May 29

Neighbors were out walking their four dogs, and we commented on how beautiful it was—sixty degrees. One wished every day was like this but then said, "It's too much to wish for. If everything in life were perfect, we might not appreciate it."

When we have been through adversity, we appreciate the better times more. God knows and is with us.

May 30

A snail was on the road today with its body outside the shell and crawling along—something I've rarely seen. On rare occasions do we let our "insides" out to be exposed. It's a relief to get something out, maybe to a friend, maybe in speaking to God. He's always there and knows what's in us, but He wants to hear it from us.

May 31

This morning I called, "Good morning," to a neighbor by name—but it was another neighbor, the neighbor in the next driveway, as he was picking up the newspaper. Whoops! I had just seen his back, as he was bent over. How many times do we do that or we are called a different name? But God knows us back, front, anytime, anywhere.

June

June 1

A plant tag, one that reads, "plant in full sunlight, water daily," was on the side of the road. Isn't that what God asks of us in baptism? To bring up our children in His full light and to water them daily in His word?

June 2

Cobwebs were buried deep in the branches of a tree, ready to catch a bug unaware. Do we see the *webs* in our everyday lives ready to snatch us up to be devoured in a way not pleasing to God? He is there to guide us around or through those *webs*.

June 3

Fences I passed this morning were made to mark boundaries, keep the unwanted out, and to be decorative. Within us, we also have fences that we use every day, hopefully for the right reasons. God is there to help use them in the way that is best for us.

June 4

A couple glided down the road on a decline and then they had to pump up the incline. I know there are times throughout the years I've been able to *glide* for a while, but then I've had to pump. Thank God for being there through the ups and downs.

June 5

The fragrance of freshly mowed grass stimulated a memory of when I was a young girl and our yard had been freshly mowed. It was then and still is a secure, fresh sense, feeling that my family

I continue to love lived in the house by that yard that we lived in. Now I also think it's a secure, refreshing, feeling that the God of love lives in me—all the time.

June 6

At the top of the driveway, sometimes I walk to the left—sometimes to the right. I just do it as the spirit drives me at the time. Because of the direction today, I saw a neighbor I hadn't seen in a while. It was good to get caught up with her doings and the neighbors around her. God keeps in touch with us, but we have to respond to Him to keep ourselves informed about what He has in mind for our daily living.

June 7

I didn't get the garbage out early enough and the pickup was earlier than usual. Therefore, when I put it out it just remained there for a longer time than usual and I thought they had missed the house. However, a follow-up truck driver came, and I was able to get it to him and wish him a good day. God provides unplanned opportunities. Thank You, God, and I pray we keep open to them.

June 8

After two days of blowing the pine straw off the driveway, it was back again this morning after a heavy wind last night. Recently I've cleaned out a few places in the house, but like the pine straw, something else fills the space. God is there to help us clear our minds daily of the clutter.

June 9

At the top of the driveway to the right, I saw four neighbors walking and joked with them that we had a "crowd and traffic jam." Jesus spoke to many crowds of all sizes and probably caused some "traffic jams." He spoke of love, peace, and joy and showed us through His actions how to live. Do we follow those actions when we meet in crowds—large or small?

June 10

A spiderweb pulled across my face along the way. I didn't see it, but it felt sticky and took several brushes with my hand to get it off. There are hidden incidents in our lives that suddenly come and "stick" to us until we can brush them away. God is there to help us get rid of them if we ask and sometimes if we don't ask. We just have to believe He's here to protect and guide us through real sticky stuff.

June 11

All sorts of chatter was going on with the birds. Do they understand each other? Are they happy, angry, planning the day? In our lives, there's a lot of daily "chatter" also. What does it mean? Are we including thanks to God for Jesus? We should.

June 12

"You're going the wrong way," a neighbor said to me, since I had reversed my lake walk from the one she usually sees. Although this morning was okay, sometimes our daily lives go the wrong way and we must pray to get back on the Jesus way.

June 13

Sunday morning unfolds with beautiful weather and neighbors to greet on the walk and thoughts about how the day may unfold. Here the world doesn't seem in a rush. There's time for church, visiting the homebound, and having someone in for dinner. Thanks to God for giving us this day to relax in His name.

June 14

"Don't bark," was the message to dogs from a neighbor on a walk. Haven't we also heard an inner voice saying not to speak or say something that's inappropriate or may offend? Do we always heed this message from God?

June 15

This morning there was a rainbow on top of greyish clouds. Then, when looking at the sunrise, the sun was sharp orange with no rays; I could look directly at it without sunglasses. There weren't shadows on the road as per usual on a sunny morning. There are predictions of rain today—thus the rainbow is a mystery. God works in mysterious ways!

June 16

The same two dogs that were being walked two days ago were also out this morning. One dog was very droopy, and the second dog was charging ahead. Will this be a droopy or charge-ahead kind of day for us? Ask God for guidance either way.

June 17

A nearby neighbor, who recently lost his wife suddenly, was walking his dog this morning. I shared his pain, since I have been through the same thing. He said it would probably get worse before better. We all go through pain at some time, but God said He wouldn't give us any more than we could bear. We have to look to Him to help us through and show us our purpose for going on in our lives.

June 18

For half of the way, no person or car passed, but suddenly a cheery home health aid came down a driveway to greet me. How blessed we are that God directs people to go into that service and that they listen.

June 19

The numerous overhead lines went unnoticed until a drop of water fell and gave me an awareness. We're a constant drop to God, and He's notices all of us, always, everywhere,

June 20

A father, mother, and two young boys came down a small hill on the road on bicycles. What fun! It's Father's Day and time for being with the family in celebration. God is our heavenly Father, but He has given us earthly fathers. I pray that fathers take their roles seriously and listen to God for guidance. *Thanks to God for the father that I had.*

June 21

The sun was full very early, as today the longest day of the year was ushered in. After dreary skies and rain it was appreciated. A bright outlook is also appreciated after dreary thoughts. Praise God for giving us sunshine.

June 22

Some driveways have gravel that helps in draining water, but deep ruts can also form. There are choices for driveway surfaces just as there are choices for our lifestyles. God is there to help direct our lifestyles.

June 23

On the side of the road was an uprooted stump. Passing it, I thought, *The roots are still there, but the branches have been cut off; it looks dead.* Even though some "branches" may be missing from our lives, God's roots are still there. Through Christ, we will find life and new "branches."

June 24

Fast runners, a slow walker, and one with a regular stride all were greeters this morning, each at a different pace. God is there to set our paces in life. May we hear Him and take Him with us on all our walks.

June 25

A black Labrador retriever came by with an iridescent lime collar that truly glowed in the dark. Do we *glow* in our dark days in God's glory? He can help us.

June 26

A garbage truck was coming, and it wasn't pickup day. It was empty, and the two men on the front seat looked to be fully enjoying themselves on the route and not picking up garbage. Do we take the opportunity God gives us to relax from work and just enjoy the day and the people around us? Ask God to help you relax.

June 27

The pace was slower with a friend as we talked. It was a good chance to really spend more time looking and discussing things we saw. Perhaps on some days we need to slow down in our lives, look around, and get a different perspective on what God has given to us.

June 28

The morning was quiet, and my mind just took in the overall beauty without singling anything out as an outstanding thought about the countryside. Thanks to God for these quiet times; it's important to know He is there even if our minds seem to be blank.

June 29

Fishermen were out and questioning if there were any fish in our lake; the answer was "Yes, just keep trying." We know there are those out in the world who can be brought to Christ by fishers of men—that is, by our actions, words, or however God chooses to use us as fishers of men. Pray for His guidance in "fishing."

June 30

Dust covered the stop sign and, except for a few clean marks, it was fuzzy. God is there to help us "stop" during whatever goes on in our lives. Just turn to Him whenever circumstances look "fuzzy" to you.

July

July 1

The day is overcast, and a few drops of rain have already fallen. Suspended drops on trees are ready for their next phase. Are we like that—suspended and waiting for our next move? God holds us just like the drops. He'll guide us to our next phase—if we let Him.

July 2

Heavy rain forced me to walk my "indoor track"—down and up stairs, alternating with circling several times around the main floor, and ending with stationary bicycling. It's marvelous how God provides an alternate course when the regular one doesn't "walk."

July 3

Clear sky, sunshine, cool breeze—what a relief after the heavy wind, rain, and tornadoes of yesterday. God does give us the beautiful day after the stormy one.

July 4

No garbage pickup today; that's what the notice said. It's a good thing God will pick up our garbage of sin and get rid of it every day when we ask. No day is a holiday for Him.

July 5

Pieces of candy were scattered here and there along the road, leftovers from yesterday's parade. We too have bits and pieces "scattered" along our roads from yesterday. They are in memories, some tossed and forgotten and some salvaged for today's activities. Pray to God that we can sort them out and go on with today.

July 6

Yellow dandelions, the unwanted—or are they? These are some of the first flowers children pick to give to Mom or someone they love. People we meet may be unwanted—maybe we feel we are, but God can use the "unwanted" to give us a chance to show love the way Jesus showed love.

July 7

A turtle crossed the road a little faster than usual when it sensed me coming. We move at our own pace too, but sometimes God urges us to go a little faster—or maybe a little slower in order for us to fulfill His will.

July 8

The family of crape myrtle was beginning to bloom along the causeway. Some bushes were full, and some hadn't started. In our lives, family members need pruning and encouragement so they can *bloom* at times according to God's plan for each, to glorify the work of Jesus Christ in us.

July 9

Everyone I met on the walk this morning had a dog, three dogs, or even five dogs. We take on responsibilities according to our interests. Let us pray that our interests include serving God's purposes and that we will be open to what those purposes are.

July 10

The sky was bright in the wide open, but where the trees were thick, I could only see it in spots. Sometimes we can see God's full purpose for us, and at other times it's spotty. We just have to keep on "walking" to get into the full "brightness" of His will.

July 11

Cool breezes filled the air—so welcome after the heat. God provides many "breezes" to help us get through uncomfortable circumstances. May we be open to them so we can be refreshed.

July 12

"Stay," commanded a lady to her three dogs as she put down their leashes in a park. If only it were that simple for us. God has given us commandments to follow and promises through His son. Listening and following the way He wants us to lead our lives will give us our fulfillment.

July 13

Rains had come earlier, and now there were threatening clouds. But a window of light in the sky provided an opportunity to make it around the three-mile lake without getting soaked. Our lives are covered with God's protection, and He will be there with His light when clouds surround us.

July 14

A neighbor was carrying a folded umbrella because the dark clouds were threatening rain again. In our "cloudy" lives, God is our umbrella, only He is always open and watching over us.

July 15

A car, a cart, and two people walking all passed me on the road at the same time; the rest of the way was clear. What serendipity to meet all at once in this uncrowded area! How many other encounters will be out there today—never to cross paths the same way? May we remember that God is with each of us as we meet, and we'll all experience our meeting differently.

July 16

It was a beautiful day, but as my thoughts drifted to tasks that had to be done, frustration set in. All of a sudden, the grass sparkled with dew as the morning sun caught it just right. God was in charge of this beauty, and these glistening drops erased my frustration.

July 17

Gray or blue skies—which will it be today? Whatever, the day is here to stay. Are events going to be gray, sunny, or a mixture? No matter what, God is with us to help us see sunshine if we prayerfully seek it.

July 18

Huge leaves were on the side of the road. Looking up, there weren't any trees matching the leaves. Did they blow there or come off a lawn care truck? Sometimes we find ourselves in an area away from our origins. Are we open to new experiences? Thank God that He follows us everywhere!

July 19

The three-mile road around the lake has many curves. One neighbor said in passing that sometimes we're going clockwise and sometimes counter clockwise as we negotiate our walk. That's like our experiences in life. Sometimes we're in sync with people one way, and other times we're going against them. God is the one who keeps us going in the right direction on our "walk" in life. Constant communication with Him gives us daily direction for our "walk."

July 20

Tiny golf balls or foil-wrapped chocolate golf balls—at least that's what they looked like to me along the causeway in the grass overlooking the golf course. Wrong! They were tiny, white mushrooms, dimples and all. How are we fooled by other things we see in this world? Jesus was sent to help us see through to the truth in what we encounter. He is the way and the truth.

July 21

Time for walking was slightly later than usual. It provided a good opportunity to see neighbors I hadn't seen in a while. One lady was hurting from an ongoing back concern, and others had their problems too. God is with us all to help with our day-to-day concerns and aging. He is an everyday constant.

July 22

There haven't been many turtles in the lake this year was my thought as I crossed the causeway. Many heads used to poke through the water in other years. Changes are always happening—sometimes we're aware of them, and other times they just slip by. But God is a constant in His love for us. That is unchanging.

July 23

One could count the drops that fell—that's how lightly it was raining. Clouds were overhead, so the bright sun wasn't showing.

However, it was getting lighter. No matter what, "clouds" and "rain" come, but Jesus, the light of the world, shines through. It may seem darker at times, but He's here to light our way.

July 24

Thud. A pinecone fell off a tree in the woods, and I heard it many feet away. God hears our every thud too, even if we're in a crowd. How blessed we are that He is everywhere, hears our "falls," and picks us up.

July 25

Turtles, bugs, a swimmer, and a fishing boat all caused ripples in their own design on the lake. However, the overall design of the ripples was caused by the wind—something not seen. In our lives we see things that cause ripples, but the most powerful force is something not seen—the Holy Spirit. It gives us our patterns for life.

July 26

When I began the walk this morning, the fog was so heavy that I could barely see the opposite shore. As soon as the sun came through, it lifted quickly. God lifts our *fog*, too—quickly at times and slowly at others. He's always there, even if we can't see the "opposite shore" immediately.

July 27

The newspaper was in an unusual place this morning, and neighbors had to search for it. Answers that come from God may be in unusual places, and we may have to search for them. However, He'll provide answers when we're ready. Sometimes we may not like them, but in the long run they'll be for our good in God's eyes for His purpose.

July 28

It was good to see a neighbor I hadn't seen lately out walking in the early morning. Our greetings were brief but sincere. How often we come in contact with people we have not seen in a while, but the same familiarity is welcome. God gives us familiarity mixed up with the new every day in order to give us food for thought. He ties our lives together with all our exchanges.

July 29

The walk was an hour later than usual. Traffic, neighbors, dogs being walked, general distance noise, and golf course maintenance equipment noise were extremely loud in combination What a difference an hour makes. God works with all of those differences in the quiet, and in the noise.

July 30

One lavender wildflower was poking up amid the low evergreen plants across the front of a yard. It added a beautiful difference. Do we dare to *pop up* and be a single, noticed entity doing God's work? Jesus did, and we can if we follow His example.

July 31

A spider was hanging down from a tall tree, on a single strand. It came out of nowhere and was getting ready to capture a bug. Suddenly, something can come out of nowhere in our lives and try to "capture" us. Are we prepared to cope with it? God is there to help us.

August

August 1

The first third of the walk, I didn't see another person or car. Then, all of a sudden, people, dogs, and vehicles were on the road. It's nice that God gives us time to be alone and time to interact with others. May we make the most of both in His name.

August 2

Rain—or not? It was that way all around the lake. Life is uncertain all the time, realize it or not. But God is a constant. He might not answer our "rain times" the way we want—but He's still there.

August 3

Up, down, curve to the right, and then curve to the left; that's the road I walk around the lake. It's also the road of life. Some are hard to climb or see around in order to anticipate what's coming. Keeping in close touch with the teachings of Jesus, we'll be able to get up and over and around all our "hills and curves."

August 4

The maintenance vehicle left tracks on the golf course. We also leave "tracks" every day. Do they show or reflect Christ's glory in our lives? Can people see or sense where we obtain our energy?

August 5

The usual walk began along the road, progressed over the causeway close to the lake, and then onto a cart path that had no golfers. Feathers of all sizes had been shed in just a short distance and I picked them up and thought of the growth they represented. In our life we grow through shedding and renewing. God is there to help us in each stage. *We just have to ask Him to guide us, listen for His guidance, and then follow it.*

August 6

My thoughts were on a presentation that I was giving today, so the walk went quickly. The school bus came by, and the children were off to their earlier-than-usual first day of school. They too were probably full of anticipation. God keeps up with all of us in preparation, anticipation, and participation. May "our anticipation" be for His glory.

August 7

Microphones they aren't, but the magnolia cores I saw on the ground looked like them. Some even had a stem on the bottom. It reminded me of years ago when I was with children on the walk and they picked these up and started talking in them as if on the radio. Funny how we can use our imaginations! But we don't have to imagine about God, for He is the real thing.

August 8

The moist golf course fairway appeared to have frost—but it was really the sun coming up behind it that caused the sparkling light to reflect. God's light behind us can cause us to sparkle too and reflect His peace and joy found in His son.

August 9

It's interesting how weeds grow through the cracks along the road. "Weeds" can also grow in the cracks of our lives if we let them. They have to be pulled from the roots and cast aside. God will be there to help pull the unwanted ones.

August 10

Small, not so obvious white cobwebs dotted the bushes along the causeway this morning, waiting for "food" to be ensnared. My thoughts drifted to how Satan is always waiting to catch us in a *web* too, and feed on us in the world. We must be aware of such *webs* and ask God to keep us from getting caught and eaten by Satan.

August 11

Lake piers: now I see one, now I don't. There's been so much rain that most of them are underwater. Last year we were under a drought, and this year we're under floods. God is definitely in control. We may not know why things happen, but He does.

August 12

I noticed the edges of the road were cracking off from the stress caused by rain. Life brings many stress factors to chip away at our edges. God sent His son to show us how to keep those edges firm.

August 13

Night sounds—I didn't even hear birds in the dark morning hours. Some animal slipped in the water, but there were no cars, people, golf course maintenance, or other human noises until halfway around; then the world started to wake up. God gives us quiet time, and He also gives us noise; each has its place. Do we respond with thanksgiving or take all of our earthly circumstances for granted.

August 14

"Mostly smooth" describes the road I walk. But if I step off, it's rough, and I must be careful. Doesn't that describe our life—mostly smooth, but rough on the side? God is there to guide our footsteps, even if we stumble.

August 15

Looking at the bushes with spiderwebs again, I was amazed that eight webs were almost covering the top of one bush. What work! How long does it take to spin a web? If we worked that hard to build God's kingdom, imagine what a world there'd be!

August 16

A dog that usually runs loose but under control with his master was on a leash with his mistress, who doesn't feel she has the same control. God lets us loose to make our choices, but sometimes we must be leashed to get back on a controlled path. Sometimes this happens through adversity meant to bring us back from running loose.

August 17

In the early morning darkness, everything was seemingly black and white—no color, just shades. The first color I noticed was the deep pink of the crape myrtle along the causeway where the sky was wide open and there was some light. God is our light, and through Him we can see His beauty in His creation.

August 18

The bright lights from an oncoming truck blocked the jogger across from me on the road who said, "Good morning." How many times does something brighter, noisier, or less important block out a quiet greeting or what God wants us to see or do? We can ask God to help us block out the interference that blocks the sight He wants us to have.

August 19

Cooler temperature this morning, but still a haze covered the sunrise; no school buses—yet—but a girl was waiting for one. Most of the way, I saw no one walking dogs—until the end when there were three, and one barked. There were no loud noises until the clang of the golf maintenance equipment. It's two experiences to a morning walk that happens. God allows us to experience two sides of our daily living. It is our choice to react to our experiences.

August 20

The crape myrtle has been a beautiful deep pine color along the causeway. Some of the blossoms are withering, and some pods have even formed, getting ready for the next season. Do we spend time getting ready for our next "season"? With God's help, we'll make the transition.

August 21

Looking into nothingness, that's what I saw, because there was thick fog across the lake. If it weren't for God being with us, our lives would be in nothingness. Thank You, God, for filling it with Your light and meaning.

August 22

Cigarette butts were strewn along one area in the pine straw along the roadway. Why do people have to clutter the roadside as well as their bodies? God made a perfect countryside, and through choice humans have messed it up. What will be our choices today? God will help us make "clean ones" where we won't mess up.

August 23

In front of one house I saw a sign that read "Protected by Central Security." That security is a comfort for those in that house. How much more comforting that our whole being is protected by God!

August 24

Even though it was dark, I recognized a neighbor by his walk. We all have characteristics that are just ours by which we are recognized. Do we portray Jesus to others in some way?

August 25

Voices I heard for the first time came from the woods where there aren't any houses. What were they doing there? Why hadn't I heard them before? We have daily questions about unusual things, and many go unanswered. We'll know about the important voices, because God is there to help identify them.

August 26

Numbers are printed many places along the walk: mailboxes, posts, doors, license plates, and phone numbers on trucks. This made me think of all the numbers that identify us on earth. God doesn't need numbers. He knows us all and can get in touch with us instantly. How refreshing!

August 27

Clear sky, cool breezes, and friendly neighbors were passing by when all of a sudden a pesky fly started buzzing around my head. There'll always be something in this life that will be irritating. What a blessing to think that the life hereafter will be perfect to those who believe God's promises. Just think, no irritations.

August 28

"What a Friend We Have in Jesus," a hymn learned in church as a child, went through my mind again and again as I walked. How comforting to know Jesus is a true friend. Who knows what the day will bring, but He'll be right here through trials and temptations.

August 29

Should I start the walk to the right or left at the top of the driveway? It depends on the time of sunrise, school buses, dogs being walked, traffic, etc. Every day we're faced with many decisions of all "sizes". Some we can make in an instant, while others take time and talking through. Thank God that He is there to guide us.

August 30

Pine straw was firmly held in the middle of the street by an invisible web. Are we not fortunate to have an invisible force—the Holy Spirit—all around and firmly holding us?

August 31

The road winds around the lake in various directions. Sometimes I can see directly into the bright sunrise, and sometimes I can't. Every day we go in different directions, and at times we might be confused. But Jesus is our light, and by that we'll find our direction.

September

September 1

It's a quiet, foggy day; even the birds were quiet this morning. Then there was a click coming from behind, and a mother and little daughter were coming on bicycles. The daughter was coming from behind, puffing to get up the small incline. She passed her mom and glided down the slight hill under her mom's careful eye. In our lives we may strive to get up our "hills" alone but then we meet God, and under His watchful eye, the move with our burdens is easier.

September 2

A light of green and light of blue were two little dots in front of the windshield on a car. Why? Who knows? There are many new things that we see each day; some we go along with, and some we pass up. Whatever is new is not always better for us. God will help us decide.

September 3

When I was almost home, a perfectly timed telephone man was at a neighbor's, so I asked him about wires coming into my house nearby a leaning tree. He stopped by and told me the identity of the wires: cable, telephone, and power. Afterward, I thought about how it's good to ask God daily to help with "wires" coming to us so they can be useful to Him in the power He has given to us.

September 4

Flashing lights and the stop arm down, the school bus was warning everyone in sight. In daily life we may have a lot of warnings for something happening, and other times we may not. One constant, Jesus, is always there to help us respond to our warning. He is our brightest light.

September 5

In the pre-dawn hours, a person who was loading a van inadvertently touched the horn button on the keys, which made the horn blare a few times. Every day we may touch some "keys" the wrong way and start something blaring. We must pray to God that we'll be sensitive to others in our communications.

September 6

Cool temperatures caused everyone I met this morning to express relief from the heat. It seems that we experience stress followed by relief in many forms throughout our lives. God allows it all and is always there to help. What a relief!

September 7

Blues and pinks blended together in the sky just before sunrise—breathtaking! A little further along, raindrops started. We never know when "raindrops" may fall in our lives, and we should always be prepared. How? Always carry God along for protection.

September 8

Gentle rain fell on the umbrella in the predawn darkness. It reminded me of the rain I heard on a tent during some camping days. How marvelous that God has given us minds with storage where memories can tie events from our lives together.

September 9

In the morning darkness a neighbor called out "Good morning" as she came for the paper. I didn't see her but recognized the voice. How blessed we are that God has given us the sense to appreciate and recognize sounds. Some may not be able to hear, and some may live where they hear bombs and guns. Thank You, God, that I could hear a neighbor's pleasant voice.

September 10

A colorful scarecrow next to colored leaves and a pumpkin were reminders that fall was coming. Of course the cooler temperatures and shortened daylight were also a clue. God gives us clues in nature and in ourselves when a transition is coming. Do we heed them?

September 11

The full moon was still out, giving light to the path, but gradually the sun rose and spread light across the sky. This is a day of mourning in the United States for the victims of the September 11, 2001, attacks, when planes were deliberately crashed in several places. However, God continues to bring His light to us in all forms. May we see it and feel its strength through any earthly tragedy.

September 12

Cloud cover prevented the moon from showing its light. Do our lives have such a *cloud cover* that God's light doesn't shine through us? Ask God to be with you to lift those clouds.

September 13

One bright light was all that was left of the millions of stars last night. The sky was pink as the sun began announcing the day, and there was just one bright light. Isn't that like Jesus, the brightest light of all, who will be there when everything else has faded?

September 14

Colorful flowers still dot the gardens along the way even though fall is settling in. One clump had velvety, pink blossoms, each blossom of which was made of tiny blossoms, and together they made up the whole. This is how God made us, with millions of parts to make up our whole. Only God knows each part of our bodies, His "temples."

September 15

The three-quarter moon had rings around it in the early hours; it looked like an eye, perhaps God's eye—beautiful! It is so comforting that God does look down on us. No matter what kind of an "eye" He uses, He's watching.

September 16

There wasn't a cloud in the sky—but the lake was covered in clouds of fog. Sometimes we may feel that above and beyond things are clear but that for now the down below is *foggy*. God will help us through the *fog*.

September 17

Wood, concrete, sand, metal, road surface, water, and other textures are all along the end of the lake near the run off. They're all different and yet are next to each other, each serving a different purpose. Each of us is different too, and though we are on the same planet, God has a specific purpose for each one of us.

September 18

Crash, bang, I heard as the blustery wind knocked down a large, dead tree limb. Often our *dead wood* has to be broken off by a blustery circumstance. Mostly it's a gradual, almost unnoticed purging. God is there to help us get rid of the unwanted day by day. How comforting!

September 19

Noise from the golf course mower obliterated the noise from a truck coming from behind that could have been in a position to strike me down. Sometimes a circumstance may cover an oncoming event that could be harmful. May we be in tune with God to keep us alert and help up with unforeseeable events.

September 20

Sparkles were on the lake where the sun hit the bugs. They are usually just seen as spots resembling raindrops. There were also sparkles penetrating the slight lake mist. The sky was blue without a cloud. God gives us sparkles in our lives, as His light shines through and glows on what might be an ordinary occurrence.

September 21

At one end of the lake I met a neighbor whose husband, who has health concerns, had gone into the hospital with a stroke. We shed tears together over the hardships. At the opposite end of the lake neighbors were walking dogs, and we commented on the beautiful weather. One said how nice it would be to have it that way all the time. After we passed, I thought *then we wouldn't appreciate this*. God is with us in all weather, and if we didn't have hardships, we wouldn't appreciate the good times as much.

September 22

There were no dog walkers and only one school bus in the early, foggy dark morning. Timing means alot in schedules when it comes to crossing paths, getting things done, and accomplishing what God wants us to do. Is today going to meet His schedule for us? He knows already.

September 23

Loud booms from a nearby military base remind us of the past and present wars. There are so many questions and so many reports. The good news is that God is in control, and in His time there will be questions answered and peace.

September 24

A school bus, maintenance truck, and a serviceman were the only three to pass by on the walk this morning. Education, maintenance of our surroundings, and protection in the world were the three things that came to mind. And who can give us guidance in these three areas the best? God!

September 25

Sunrise in clouds through the pines and over the moist, white golf course was truly a picture. Many paintings have depicted sunrises in much the same surroundings. None can compare to what God has given to us in living color.

September 26

There were still many stars out this morning, brightly shining. However, as the sky lightened from the oncoming sun, the stars faded. Our lives are filled with "stars" here and there, but God's light is brighter. All of those individual lights fade as God fills us with His light.

September 27

Another Saturday morning and the weather is beautiful. People are gradually moving and not quite as rushed as they are on weekdays. It's so nice to have a slowed atmosphere to absorb the beauty God has provided. Thank goodness He has given us down time—if only we could all take advantage of it and not be caught up in so much worldly busyness.

September 28

A diverted path off the main road led to a gravel road. Off to the left were a small lake and a house. All around the path and road were posted signs warning, "no trespassing," so turning to the main road was the only option. Do we have "no trespassing" signs around us so people can't come to us for help? God works through us to help other people. Are we open to helping their needs? Pray God will guide us in how to help others.

September 29

Trees are mostly in bunches where they blend together. A single tree stands out. In the early hours, when the sky lightens before the sun rises, this is very noticeable. In life there are crowds, and then there are people who stand out one way or another. No matter, for God loves us all as individuals. He has a plan for each, but we have to listen to Him and not outside influences.

September 30

How refreshing the newly fallen pine straw looks against the old, dried out straw covering the yards. Every day we can also refresh ourselves by turning to God and asking Him to give us a renewed spirit to do His will. We too can have fresh "straw" cover us.

October

October 1

When crossing the causeway in the fog this morning, I saw the golf maintenance mower had a light on the front guiding the driver in his task. We too need a light guiding us in our "foggy" lives, and that light is Christ, who is always there. Even in the sunshine, He'll "shine" brighter as He guides our way.

October 2

Timer on. That must be the reason a neighbor's sprinkler system was on in the dark morning hours. Do we have timers on too—and all the time—to hear God talking to us, to automatically *turn on* to doing His will? Or do we wait until Sunday mornings to listen to Him?

October 3

Another squirrel was dead on the road, one of several I've seen this week. Is it because they're scurrying about in order to store up food for the winter and not paying attention to their instincts? Do we scurry about in our daily activities and not pay attention to God's warnings about consequences? Being too busy is an easy "invitation" to being hit unexpectedly.

October 4

Trees were dripping in the woods, the residual from last night's rain. At first it seemed it was raining, but since there weren't drops coming I knew what I was hearing wasn't rain. When we hear bad things about people is it for real, or is it just residual gossip? God tells us to love, not gossip. Can we redirect our gossip to love? God can help us.

October 5

A mixed up light configuration was gleaming its orange light in the dark this morning. Halloween is coming, so maybe that was related to its significance. God's light is always there for us—night and day. Sometimes we may be mixed up in our minds about how to follow it, but if we turn our days to Him, He'll show us the way.

October 6

A little neighbor girl was trying to catch her pet black rabbit in a bucket this morning. It was running toward the road, so I tried to chase it back. The girl tried with the bucket but missed. Her brother and mother were calling her to get into the van for school. Finally the girl said with confidence, "That's all right. She'll be okay," so I went on. When we turn things over to God, do we think it'll be all right and just keep going? That's okay, we should!

October 7

A whole mile, and no people or vehicles were on the road. Then over the causeway were a truck and two neighbors with three dogs; a little further was an oncoming car, and I had thoughts of crossing over from the shoulder. Then, all of a sudden, a car was coming in that direction, followed by a school bus. There was a driveway to help me get further off to the side. God does provide help for us to get off the "road" when life becomes too full of potential danger.

October 8

A single leaf was on the road this morning with no stones, sticks, or other leaves by it. How many times are we alone, or at least feel we are? God is with us to give us company and direction. Just ask Him.

October 9

Crossing the causeway one half hour after official sunrise, I saw the light sifting through the lengthened clouds and reflecting in the lake—gorgeous! But, to the far right, there was a peek of the colors of the rainbow; the sun must have caught some moisture. It was what God gave to Noah—a promise of hope, which is what He gives to us in Jesus Christ. What a great way to the start of a busy day—the beauty of an ongoing promise that He'll always be with us.

October 10

The morning dark was beautiful with a sliver of the moon and a few stars sifting through the clouds. The newspaper deliverers passed me by, and then I caught up with another early morning walker; we talked until he was home. It's so nice to start the day casually being with people in God's world. Thank You, God.

October 11

Wind chimes blowing in the gentle wind greeted me this morning before sunrise. There weren't any vehicles or people until the halfway mark, and then a few trucks, cars, and people walking dogs were there. Every day might be like that, with only the calm wind at first and then busyness. We don't know who or what is going to cross our paths, but God does and is with us.

October 12

In the early, dark morning, a car pulled out of a driveway, and the driver said hello to me. Further on down, a couple was walking three dogs, and we exchanged greetings. Two trucks passed by and blinked their lights. I didn't see any of the usual people, but God was there giving me "food" through these people in setting the tone for the day.

October 13

As I walked out the door, there were stars in part of the sky. Going a bit further, heat lightening was flashing. The hymn "Softly and Tenderly" came to mind and stayed with me the whole way around. Except for a few drops of rain, no storm came. Although I don't like storms, even heat lightening, and sometimes feel anxious over them, my spirit was calm. I kept focused on the hymn and thought Jesus was spreading His light to me in those flashes.

October 14

Clouds were thick, so I couldn't see the sunrise this morning. However, by the end of the walk, the sky was blue with fluffy white clouds, and the sun's reflections were lighting up the area. Sometimes our "clouds" are so thick that we can't see the "light," but with prayer and faith, Christ's light shines through.

October 15

Light rain was falling this morning, which made the dark surfaced roads in the open reflect light greater than the dry roads. The light of Christ can shine brighter on our "dark" paths also. Thank You, God, for those bright spots in our "dark" times.

October 16

It feels like a Saturday. There were no school buses or vans rushing to school with children, and only a few pickup trucks were going to work. The weather was clear with just a small breeze, the sky was free of dark clouds, and the sun was coming up to lighten and warm the day. Thank You, God, for this peace after a busy week.

October 17

The sun was in its fullness, and one could not look right at it without being *blinded*. However, the reflections on the frosty golf course and the fog steam rising from the lake were magnificent! If we look right into the full light of Christ, it might be too much all at once, but His reflections all around are indeed magnificent. Let's take it all in and help others to do likewise.

October 18

The dog looked familiar, but where was its master? Soon a voice coming from behind determined that. In that brief encounter along the walk, we became acquainted. It's strange how God sends even dogs to lead the way, break the ice.

October 19

Reflections of the houses and trees from the opposite shore were on the lake. However, in between there was a strong current whose ripples caused a disfiguration of those houses and trees. We can have a strong reflection of Christ in our lives, but we must be careful that daily circumstances don't distort it. I pray that God will help our images be true to His word.

October 20

Suddenly in the early dark, a few red lights came on next to me; a truck started its motor, pulled out of the driveway, and passed by. That startled me because I was caught off guard. Many times we're caught off guard and are startled until we regain our composure. It's a lesson in being aware of what's going on around us and thanking God for being there to help.

October 21

There are different sounds on the walk: trucks, airplanes, maintenance equipment for the golf courses, various bird calls, other walkers talking, dogs barking, footsteps. Throughout a day, we also hear people talking. Sometimes it's chatter, but other times the meaning is deeper; are we really hearing the message? Through the example of God's love and His guidance, we can pray to understand and then react in love.

October 22

The sky was thick with clouds this morning, but streaks of pink light showed the sun coming. Further along I looked back, and sure enough it was out in beautiful pinkish orange. Even if our day starts out cloudy, we can pray that sunshine will show through—even if it's just a little. *Have faith*, we're told, *even small as a mustard seed*.

October 23

The police stopped and asked me if I had seen a lost little white dog. "No, not so far." On the other side of the lake one was darting across the road. With the help of a neighbor, I picked it up and then another neighbor walking a dog gave me a leash. When home I called the police; then the woman who was looking came by and then the police. What timing! If happiness so obvious can exist when a lost dog is found, imagine how God feels when a person is found in His name!

October 24

Tiny bubbles formed on top of the water that was running on the other side of the road. Then all of a sudden one would break. Do we have "bubbles" in our lives that seem unusual and worth carrying along in our stream of dreams? Do they break? Are we bothered by their bursting, or do we dismiss them and think there must be a reason? God knows the reason and tells us to keep going.

October 25

The sky was black with a thick cloud cover. One bright beam did flash by quite often, however, from the nearby airport. How comforting for pilots headed that way. We have the promised light from Jesus all the time. What a comfort that is!

October 26

The stars were bright, and I noticed the Big Dipper that points to the North Star, a guide that points to the north no matter what. God through the Holy Spirit is our constant guide in our lives. Do we look to Him for our direction no matter what?

October 27

I heard scuffling footsteps down a driveway as garbage bags were brought to the front. How easy it is to get rid of garbage. What's even easier is to pray to God to get rid of our "garbage." He's there to forgive our sins and to set us on a non-garbage course according to His will.

October 28

Camellias are blooming just when many other things in the landscape are changing colors, dying, and blowing around. There is a time and season for everything. God sees to that. Where will I *bloom* and *die* today?

October 29

Small pods on long stems stuck out from the fall-colored leaves on the crape myrtle bushes along the causeway. It was as if to say that they're just as important as the purple blossoms that once filled the branches. But those blossoms had to die and pods had to form to ready for their next season. God planned it that way just as He plans that something in us must die in order to prepare our next season for growth.

October 30

A spider loomed in front of me and was seemingly in midair, but it was suspended from a high branch. Do we feel as if we're hanging by a thread sometimes? Just as God made the spider's thread strong, He can also make our "threads" strong. If we come to Him, we have His support whether we see it or not.

October 31

"It's a spectacular day with the sun shining through the fog over the lake." So said a young serviceman neighbor as he jogged past me. He always has a positive slant on the day when we pass in the morning. God gives us so many reasons to be joyful. Let us share them as the neighbor does.

November

November 1

The morning was still dark, even after we set the clocks back this weekend. It's funny how we expect things to be different in our thinking, but most of the time they aren't. God knows how light and dark it's going to be, just as He knows where each life is heading. Trust Him to hold it together, no matter the changes.

November 2

"Yes, Jesus Loves Me" was going through my mind on the walk this beautiful morning. How comforting to know that no matter how busy God is in taking care of all His world, He doesn't give up loving and caring for each of us.

November 3

The leaves crackled underneath my feet, which reminded me of a carefree childhood playing in the autumn leaves. God was there then when the leaves crackled, and He was here today when they crackled. This is a reminder that although things seem to change, His world is intact; the coming and going of seasons is evidence of that.

November 4

A flashing red light was an alert to me for something—in this case a dog walker. How many flashing red lights do we see in a day on the street and in our heads? We're given warning signals in different ways. Do we heed them? Do we ask God to help us safely through them? He's there; just ask Him.

November 5

The fog was so thick that the form of the opposite shore wasn't even visible to me. Then a car came toward me a short distance on the causeway, and I could see the lights. Christ's light shines through anything, any *fog* we may experience. How blessed we are to have that light.

November 6

Looking into the woods, I judged that within a ten-foot area there were at least ten different kinds of trees and bushes—and that's just the minimum number of different trees and bushes found in other areas. They are all living together in one soil, just as God put them there. Wouldn't it be peaceful if people could live by each other like this? God promised we would be together in eternity.

November 7

A moving line that looked like it was caused by something moving underwater was just a long weed floating—an illusion. How often we are faced with illusions, which is a good reason not to judge or jump to conclusions. God is the only judge; let Him handle it.

November 8

Harry, a familiar neighborhood dog, was on the street as the walk began. Apparently his master wasn't around, so I decided to take him to his house. He followed willingly, and when we got close he ran right up and inside since the door was ajar. How many of us have the faith to run to God who will take us in. All we have to do is believe that the door will be open.

November 9

A cold wind penetrated the morning, yet I noticed the far end of the lake was calm compared to this end. It's comforting to turn to God to keep us calm in rough waters when there is a strong wind—even if it seems too rough in the daily "waters" for other people.

November 10

The moon was full, the sky was without clouds, the sun was coming up, and the air was almost freezing. All of this beauty from God was stimulating to me. Even though all of the above are constantly changing in various seasons, they're still there. God is in charge of their temperaments, just as He is in our "seasons"—if we ask Him and remain patient for His answer.

November 11

Suddenly a squirrel darted across the top of a thin fence with assurance. I thought, *imagine being so agile and sure!* God made it that way just as He's made us gifted and has given us the assurance that He's always with us, even if we fall. He's there to pick us up if we want. How comforting!

November 12

All of nature has something in common: outsides that can be seen and insides that can't be seen unless cut open. However, humans have souls that the rest of nature doesn't have, and even if we're cut open, our souls can't be seen. They're part of us, and they determine our relationships with other humans and with God. He blesses our souls with the Holy Spirit that will guide us in our everyday dealings if we ask and then listen to His directives.

November 13

Very windy describes the early morning. It's strange how something we can't see—only feel—can cause storms, leaves and branches to fall, fires to rage, waters to churn, clouds to whip on, and cool comfort on a hot day. I thought this morning of how God promised to be with us to help calm us in our "wind" and bring us comfort and relief.

November 14

The sky was a brilliant deep-to-light pink this morning in the east just before I saw the sun peek. Breathtaking! After the sun rose, the rest of the sky and clouds were light pinks. It was as if the beauty had to be shared. Isn't that our relationship to Christ? He has the light and beauty for us to see and feel, but He wants us to spread that beauty and light by sharing it with others through actions, words, and prayers.

November 15

The lake was like a mirror to me, with the only apparent motion coming from the clouds. However, there's motion under the water, to be sure. We may meet people who are calm on the outside, and we think all is okay—but they may not be okay in their insides. We can pray that God will help us calm those insides and that He will also help calm our insides when we need it.

November 16

Birds were squawking along the treetops lining the causeway. There was a lot of flying activity too, and I could see twelve, fifteen—even twenty birds, each sitting on a top branch. They were looking toward the lake as if in worship and full appreciation of the beauty before them. Do we sit on the "treetops" in our lives in worship and appreciation of the beauty God has created for us?

November 17

Missing from my walk this morning were a couple and their three dogs for whatever reason. How many times do we expect something that doesn't happen? As promised, though, we can always expect God to be there. We can count on it, whether we recognize Him or not.

November 18

Startled from my walking by, three ducks flew out from the wall hiding their presence on the causeway. After landing in the water, they settled down and seemed to lose their anxiety, knowing they wouldn't be hurt. Don't we get startled, too, and fill with anxiety? Thank God we can ask Him to calm and protect us from scary circumstances.

November 19

Umbrella up and umbrella down, winds calm then blustery, rain heavy, no rain—I was experiencing very unpredictable weather this morning. Lives are unpredictable too. We don't know what's going to happen to us in the near future, even in the next few minutes, but God does. He is there to be our umbrella and shield us through blustery times and blustery minutes. Just ask Him.

November 20

The fall season is over, and leaves were down from the thick stands of trees. Now I could see beyond to the lake. Sometimes the "leaves" are too thick in our lives, and we have to clear them out to see beyond. This season is over, and now God has plans for our next one. His Holy Sprit will be there to guide us when things seem too thick to see beyond.

November 21

Thank goodness for the streetlight still being on before the sensors turned them off. Although I had a flashlight and the sun was just beginning to give light, the extra light was appreciated. With Jesus, we don't have to worry about His light going out, for He is the true light of the world that is always there to light our way.

November 22

The sky was clear, with a tinge of pink from the sunrise. I saw ducks flying high above with wings fluttering madly. How powerful God made them for their flights. God also made us powerful for living in the world, and we are made to do things in His name we never thought we had the power to do.

November 23

A yellow ribbon was stretched across a newly resurfaced driveway that could be ruined if someone stepped on it. As a contrast, Christ asked us to come right to Him, where we will be made new. We don't have to worry about being *stepped on*. He is there to keep us new and safe.

November 24

Loading and unloading and shifting from one place to another were activities I observed about some neighbors this morning. We load and unload and shift things that come into our lives daily—physically, mentally, and spiritually. Thanks to God, we have Him to turn to when we have burdens loaded on us and need help unloading or shifting them about.

November 25

The birds weren't chirping much at first, and then it sounded like the birds all around the lake were together in one meeting place, all chirping. After passing by and walking way down the road, I couldn't hear them. What was in them to cause the commotion? What's in us to cause it at times? God knows, and He'll be there to calm us—if not now, then down the road.

November 26

The streetlights were few and the morning was dark, even with my flashlight. A car with a newspaper deliveryman inside was parked under one light while he readied the papers. He needed that light just as we need Jesus to be our everyday light, especially in our darkness and struggles.

November 27

An emergency vehicle and a police car were parked out in front of my neighbor's house in the dark morning hours. We never know when an emergency will happen, but God is there to give direction. Just ask Him, and He'll take care of our concerns.

November 28

The predictions I heard for rain yesterday, last night, and this morning never held true. We can't predict anything accurately; only God knows what's going to happen. Therefore, our minds should be kept open to Him.

November 29

The tops of the pine trees were glowing from the sun that came up a short time ago. This contrasted with the darkness of the trees below. It reminded me of a woman who was disabled in her lower body yet was always glowing with a smile. She loved her Lord, and it showed.

November 30

Some of the many reflections I saw this morning were on the lake, curbs, driveways, trees, and vehicles. However, something had to come to each of these in order to reflect. Similarly, Christ has to come to each of us for us to reflect Him to others. He's ready to come when we ask Him.

December

December 1

The lake had two kinds of ripples on it—at least it looked like that. One had large ripples, and beyond they were small; it depended on the wind. Isn't our life like that? Sometimes we have large ripples of activities and emotions, and just beyond that we also have smaller ones. God knows them all and can help us counteract any wind.

December 2

Crossing over the causeway, I can see the lake on one side and the golf course on the other. The contrast of the shinning, reflecting water with the dark, solid earth is a reminder that God provides all kinds of contrasts in our lives too. He gives us options, and the choices we make to reflect Him are up to us.

December 3

The early sunrise was a pink glow that dotted the clouds. It doesn't happen that way often, so I appreciate it when it does. Thanks to God for that glow and also the glow that He gives to us. Conditions may be such that we don't have it all the time, but when it's there, it's really appreciated. Thank You, God.

December 4

The heavy cloud cover prevented me from seeing where the sun was rising; it was just getting lighter in general. Christ gives us light throughout. We can't identify His exact spot—but He's there.

December 5

The rain is finished, but the streets are still wet. Some dry areas are showing around the cracks, and I wonder if the earth's heat coming through those cracks causes the drying. Isn't that possible with us also? We may feel saturated with problems, but gradually they can be *dried out* as we let God's warmth enter us or we open ourselves to Him.

December 6

The posts along the causeway are about the same size; the tops slant alike and have the same weathered look, as well. At closer glance, they are different in knots, grain, texture, etc. Yet, they all serve the same purpose. We may all be clumped together as humans, but we're all so different with different gifts. Yet, our purpose is the same—to glorify God in using our talents.

December 7

Walking out the door this morning, I could hear something flitting high in the carport. It was still dark, but a bird (or a bat) was flying near the ceiling and hitting the wide eaves as if trying to escape. At last it found freedom. Don't we flit about at times, trying to find ourselves out of a situation? God promises that if we turn it over to Him, we can be free from the worry and anguish.

December 8

The morning is beautiful with the full moon, but because of an early scheduled meeting, I did not walk the whole way. However, life goes on—the moon still sets and the sun rises as God fulfills His schedule. He's in charge of it all.

December 9

This morning I saw the moon, sunrise, clear sky, fog, and then the light from a lone Christmas tree on a dock across the lake. Usually there are many Christmas trees with colored lights on even in the morning, but this one was alone and all white, just as Jesus is the one special light that comes to us. He is pure, as in all white. May we focus on only Him coming through the *fog* in our lives.

December 10

The rain wasn't to come until this afternoon, but the drops started falling halfway around the lake. As is stated in the Bible, only God knows what's going to happen when. The sun will come again, just as the sun will come to our lives if we are going through "rain."

December 11

Rounding the corner at the causeway, I could see the lake had a border of posts and bushes that formed a series of regular designs that combined into a shape like a square window with a lake view. At closer range, those designs weren't so even. At first glimpse, they may seem the same, but at closer view, they aren't. God has made us all different, but He loves us equally. Christ gave His life for all.

December 12

The moon looked like a bright football. Imagine: God planned this whole universe, even with the moon reflecting off the sun, and its fullness restarts every month. It's never missed. How amazing God has time for my details, too. Thanks be to God!

December 13

Puffy clouds filled the sky. In occasional breaks, a star and the moon would peek through. In our lives, we have occasional breaks where opportunities peek through to serve God. Let's make the most of them.

December 14

Signs reading "No Outlet" and "Dead End" are on one of the side roads. Do we see these "signs" in everyday life and heed them? Thanks to God, Jesus Christ is our outlet before we reach a "dead end."

December 15

There's sand in spots along the side of the road that in early dark morning looks like snow. It's funny how our imaginations can pull tricks. But God is no trick. He is real and everywhere.

December 16

In the morning dark, everything is seen in an outline—nothing shows depth yet. Isn't that the way we see people for the first time? When we get to know them, we go deeper. God has always gone deeper. He sees into our hearts. Let's always pray to Him to help us cleanse the depths of our hearts daily.

December 17

There was a slight rain, but the moon was out to give light. Isn't that true in our lives? Even though we may have some "rain," Christ gives light to see our way through the "rain" and "dark" to the light.

December 18

The pink sky was brilliant as I started my walk, and my thoughts were on a beautiful sunrise. Then gray clouds covered the sky, and the anticipated sunrise was covered. Our daily lives may start out full of glorious anticipation, and then clouds may come in to change our experience. God is with us no matter how our anticipations of a glorious day may change, even if there's a cloud cover.

December 19

The morning was overcast, and the rain started close to home. Maybe snow flurries are to come later—who knows? Only God. What we do know, however, is that He'll be there through rain, snow, sunny skies—night and day. We may not be prepared, but He is!

December 20

The morning was clear, but there were a few puddles from last night's rain. One such puddle held leaves, pine needles, and other debris floating in a beautiful collage-like arrangement. As God makes use of something that we might rake up and toss away, so too He uses people who might feel unworthy to serve His purposes. To Him all people have worth; we just have to be open to His direction for our purposes.

December 21

The late morning was beautifully bright, clear, and brisk; one needed a hood on. What a difference the bright sun makes after gray clouds and cold wind, just as the light of Jesus makes a difference in one's life after *life's clouds and cold wind*.

December 22

A few Christmas lights were still on, their twinkles piercing the early dark, just like stars piercing the sky. However, lights have to be hung on something, but stars "hang" on their own as God planned, just as we have to be on our own with God. He will help us "hang in there."

December 23

A cigarette wrapper or box was on the side of the road—an intrusion in God's beautiful natural setting. People toss out trash just as they do gossip—freely. May we realize how unbecoming and potentially harmful these thoughtless ways are. Let us ask God to help us handle such situations His way when we face them.

December 24

Many people were out walking, even though rain was predicted. After hearing about all the rushing for last-minute Christmas preparations, it was so nice to wish "Merry Christmas" to people taking the time to enjoy God's nature.

December 25

It was a beautiful Christmas morning, but my thoughts kept turning to the guests who were coming in two hours for brunch and the fact that some preparations still had to be made. All of a sudden, I realized that those preparations were being made too important and that the true meaning of Christmas was in the background. A "Merry Christmas" from other walkers was a reminder of that true meaning. May we ask God for forgiveness for sometimes forgetting what He has given to us.

December 26

The morning after Christmas was spent with others in another location. The walk was peaceful, even though it included passing houses closer together, moving along and then crossing a busier street, and walking by a small shopping strip and through a playground area. God gives us new areas to explore and then is there to guide us through them.

December 27

The trees were coated from the weekend snow of three feet, five inches. It looked like a can of whipped cream was used to line the branches and needles of the pines and other trees. The whole scene was beautiful. Thank You, God, for providing all sorts of beautiful sights.

December 28

Two squirrels were running in opposite directions across the road in front of me as I walked. That's life. Many people go in opposite directions of our lives. We all have different reasons for running the way we do. The important thing is that we're going in the direction that God shows us. May we be open to that direction.

December 29

The day was calm, cold, and beautifully clear. All of a sudden, there were gunshots through the woods in the hunting area. I imagined living in a war torn area and wondered how people manage to live in that fear. God is with everyone, but here it's easy compared to wherever there is war. Thank You, God, for the absence of war, and for being with those who are facing it.

December 30

The morning rain was on and off, just like the "rain" in our lives. An umbrella protects us from the raindrops, but God protects us from our individual lives' "raindrops." The inward peace and sun that comes from God truly surpass all understanding.

December 31

Stepping off the road is easy, and it is felt immediately. In our lives, we step off the paths that God intended for us, and we can feel the difference. Thanks be to God that we can quickly get back on and ask His forgiveness and guidance to do His will and to keep us on the main road.